Fred. S. Goodman

Main Lines in the Bible

A Short Course of Introductory Bible Studies....

Fred. S. Goodman

Main Lines in the Bible
A Short Course of Introductory Bible Studies....

ISBN/EAN: 9783337246747

Printed in Europe, USA, Canada, Australia, Japan

Cover: Foto ©Lupo / pixelio.de

More available books at **www.hansebooks.com**

MAIN LINES IN THE BIBLE

A SHORT COURSE OF

INTRODUCTORY BIBLE STUDIES

FOR

CLASSES AND PERSONAL USE

ESPECIALLY IN

RAILROAD
YOUNG MEN'S CHRISTIAN
ASSOCIATIONS

PREPARED BY

FRED. S. GOODMAN

NEW YORK
THE INTERNATIONAL COMMITTEE OF YOUNG MEN'S
CHRISTIAN ASSOCIATIONS

CONTENTS.

INTRODUCTION .... Pages 4, 5

THE BOOK.

Lesson I.—What it is........................ 6

Lesson II.—How we got it.................. 9

OUR GOD.

Lesson III.—The Father 12

Lesson IV.—The Exalted Son.............. 14

Lesson V.—The Ever-present Helper......... 16

THE MAN.

Lesson VI.—What he is and what he ought to be 18

Lesson VII.—His needs—(1) Forgiveness.... 21

Lesson VIII.—(2) A new heart.............. 24

Lesson IX.—(3) The new life............... 26

Lesson X.—The Saved Man's Training—(1) Prayer 28

Lesson XI.— (2) Bible study 30

Lesson XII.— (3) Service 34

Lesson XIII.—His glorious future........... 37

Lesson XIV.—Review 40

List of Books........................... 42

INTRODUCTION.

This course of lessons has been prepared at the request of the International Committee to meet the special needs of railroad men. A large majority of these men are deprived of facilities or opportunities for thorough or consecutive Bible study. For this reason the usual graded courses are not available for most of them. In the judgment of some who are familiar with the needs of this great body of men, especially those who are in touch with Railroad Young Men's Christian Associations, there seems to be a need for a short, simple, comprehensive, and yet practical course of studies, so arranged as to be adapted to the man who can only snatch a few moments here and there, as well as to the man whose time and inclinations permit a larger amount of study.

The title, "Main Lines in the Bible," indicates its general character. The lessons are simply a few starting points in the vast realm of Bible truth. Any one of them might profitably occupy as many lessons as the course provides. It is hoped that many men may make beginning towards a thorough study of these great themes through their use of this necessarily fragmentary treatment.

It is suggested that those who study the course pursue the following method, more or less fully according to the time at their disposal. The points are presented in the order of their importance.

1. Learn the Memory Text.

2. Read carefully the Daily Readings. This will take not to exceed six minutes a day.

3. Read thoughtfully the questions and answers, especially the portions of scripture printed in black-faced type. Read them over several times.

4. Look up in your own Bible the references suggested, but not printed in full. These might be largely increased in number.

The Daily Readings have been selected with much care. The leader will do well to assign the various readings to different members of the class, and ask each one to come prepared to give the central thought of the reading assigned him. It will be well, also, to ascertain each week how many have followed the readings during the previous week. By thus calling attention to them their importance will be emphasized. Through their use many men may be led to form the very important habit of daily Bible reading.

Every member of the class should possess his own Bible, and in addition a copy of the Revised Version of the New Testament. There is economy in getting a well printed and well bound Bible. The author recommends on page 42 what he regards as an excellent low-priced book for men in railroad service.

MAIN LINES IN THE BIBLE.

STUDY HINTS.

1. Commit the "Memory Text" on the first day, and recall it frequently during the week.
2. Try to look up every text in your own Bible. This will help to fix the location in mind and make you familiar with the book.
3. Be regular in using the daily readings, even though you are obliged to miss any class session.
4. Do not be discouraged with slow progress. The Bible deserves the study of a life time. To simply learn the Memory Text will prove of great value.
5. Use or refer to the Revised Version of the New Testament (see page 42). It will frequently lighten up a difficult or familiar text. The initials "R. V." in the book refer to the Revised Version.
6. Always remember that the division of the Bible into chapters and verses is not found in the original copies of the Bible. It is of comparatively modern origin. The Revised version follows a paragraph arrangement, which usually makes the sense more clear by showing the setting and context of the various verses.
7. The blank pages are inserted to make it easy to take notes. Original work of this kind is of great value.

LESSON I.

The Book. What It Is.

DAILY READINGS.

First Day........................Psalm 119:9-24
Second Day......................Psalm 119:89-104
Third Day.......................Psalm 119:105-120
Fourth Day........................Luke 24:13-27
Fifth Day.........................Luke 24:28-53
Sixth Day..........................Acts 17:1-12
Seventh Day......................Isaiah. 55:1-13

MEMORY TEXT.

"I have esteemed the words of his mouth more than my necessary food." Job 23:12.

1. What are some of the common names given to this book?

   (1) *The Bible,* (2) *The Word,* (3) *The Scriptures.*

2. What is the meaning and significance of each of these names?

   (1) *"The Bible" comes from a Greek word which originally meant "the books." Later it became "the book" through the Latin. First used in the fourth century after Christ.*

   (2) *"The Word"—Words are instruments for conveying thought. The Bible is God's instrument for letting men know his thought regarding them.*

   See Acts 20:32. **"And now, brethren, I commend you to God and to the word of his grace, which is able to build you up and give you an inheritance."**
   Psalm 119:162. **"I rejoice at thy word as one that findeth great spoil."**

   (3) *"The Scriptures" comes from a Latin word meaning "the writings." The Bible was only in written form until the invention of printing in the fifteenth century. The first complete book printed was a Bible.*

   See Rom. 15:4. **"Whatsoever things were written aforetime were written for our learning that we, through patience and through comfort of the scriptures, might have hope."** See also 2 Tim. 3:16.

3. What are some of its figurative titles found in the Bible?

   A lamp (Psalm 119:105), *a hammer (Jeremiah* 23:29), *a sword (Ephesians* 6:17), *milk (I Peter* 2:2), *seed (Luke* 8:11).

4. How is the book made up and divided?

   Of sixty-six separate books or parts, divided into two main sections called the Old and the New Testaments.

5. How may we divide the Old Testament?

Into three parts—(1) History, (2) Poetry, (3) Prophecy.

6. How many books in each?

1. *History*	*Books of Moses.... 5* *Later Books.......12*	17
2. *Poetry*	*Job, Psalms, Proverbs Ecclesiastes, Song of Solomon ....*	5
3. *Prophecy*	*Greater Prophets... 5* *Lesser Prophets....12*	17
		39 *Books*

7. How divide the New Testament?

1. *History*	*Matthew, Mark, Luke, John, Acts.........*	5
2. *Letters*	*Paul's Letters......14* *General Letters.... 7*	21
3. *Prophecy*	*Revelation ....*	1
		27 *Books*

8. What makes these sixty-six books one book?

They have a common origin—the purpose of God—and a common theme, man and his relations to God and his fellow-men, as they have been and ought to be.

9. What is the pervading purpose of the book?

To teach men of God, and how to please Him, and thus accomplish their own highest good.

See Psalm 19:7-11. "The testimony of the Lord is sure, making wise the simple. The judgments of the Lord are true and righteous altogether. Moreover by them is thy servant warned, and in keeping of them there is great reward." See also 1 Cor. 10:11.

10. How should men receive and treat the Book?

As a personal message from the Almighty God.

See 1 Thess. 2:13. "**When ye received the word of God . . . ye received it not as the word of men, but as it is in truth, the word of God. which effectually worketh also in you that believe.**" See also Luke 8:9-15, James 1:16-25.

NOTE: Have the class turn to these last two references and read them aloud together in closing the session.

SUGGESTIONS TO THE LEADER.

1. Look up in the class all the references which are not printed in full.

2. Have all questions answered from memory. Avoid reading the answers in the class.

3. Spend five to ten minutes on questions 6 and 7 in a drill in the number and order of the books. Do this also at the opening of each of the next three lessons. It will help to fix permanently in mind the simple division of books suggested.

4. Open and close each lesson with prayer. Select in advance one of the members to close the lesson, that he may pray thoughtfully and in line with the teachings of the hour.

5. Avoid unprofitable discussion. Let the Scriptures make their own appeal to the hearts of the men.

LESSON II.

The Book. How We Got It.

DAILY READINGS.

First Day........................... Psalm 19:1-14
Second Day.................. Deuteronomy 31:14-30
Third Day........................... Joshua 1:1-9
Fourth Day...................... 2 Samuel 23:1-17
Fifth Day.......................... Mark 12:18-37
Sixth Day...................... 2 Timothy 3:1-17
Seventh Day...................... 2 Peter 1:13-21

MAIN LINES IN THE BIBLE.

MEMORY TEXT.

"**The prophecy came not of old time by the will of man, but men spake from God, being moved by the Holy Ghost.**" 2 Peter 1:21, R. V.

1. How many different men were engaged in writing the Book?

   The number is unknown. There were at least thirty.

2. Name twelve leading writers.

   (1) *Moses*, (2) *David*, (3) *Solomon*, (4) *Ezra*, (5) *Isaiah*, (6) *Jeremiah*, (7) *Ezekiel*, (8) *Matthew*, (9) *Mark*, (10) *Luke*, (11) *John*, (12) *Paul.*

3. During how long a period was the book written?

   About sixteen hundred years. The Old Testament about eleven hundred years, or from 1500 *B. C. to* 400 *B. C. The New Testament from about* 60 *to* 95 *A. D.*

4. In what languages were the various books written?

   The Old Testament almost wholly in Hebrew. The New Testament in Greek.

5. How has the Bible come down to our time?

   By means of carefully written copies of the original documents. There are now in existence several hundred manuscript copies more or less complete, a few going back to within 200 *years of the death of the last writer.*

6. When was the first English translation made?

   That by John Wycliffe about 1380 *A. D. It was a translation of the Vulgate or old Latin Version, which goes back to* 385 *A. D. The first complete copy in English was that by Coverdale, published in* 1535.

7. What two later English versions are of special interest to us?

   The so-called King James Version, completed in 1611 *A. D.—the one now in common use—and the Revised Version completed in* 1885.

8. Why is the Revised Version valuable?

It gives a more accurate and modern translation of the original text, because of the advance in biblical scholarship, and the discovery of several very early manuscripts unknown when the King James Version was published.

9. What should be the chief aim in reading and studying the Book?

To learn of the character of God, and to discover how to so live as to please and honor Him, best serve our fellow men, and enjoy God's favor forever.

"Thy word have I hid in my heart that I might not sin against thee." Psalm 119:11.

"These are written that ye may believe that Jesus is the Christ, the Son of the living God, and that believing ye may have life in his name." John 20:31, R. V.

10. What are necessary characteristics of a successful Bible student?

(1) *Earnestness.* Acts 17:11. Jer. 29:13.

(2) *Obedience.* James 1:21-27.

(3) *Prayerfulness.* Psalm 119:18.

(4) *Faith.* Hebrews 11:6.

11. What benefits will follow earnest, obedient, believing study?

(1) *Spiritual growth.* 1 Peter 2:2. Acts 20:32.

(2) *A cleaner life.* Psalm 119:9-11.

(3) *Knowledge and wisdom.* Psalm 119:104. 2 Tim. 3:15.

(4) *Satisfaction.* Jer. 15:16. Psalm 119:103.

(5) *Moral courage.* Joshua 1:8, 9.

(6) *Victory over evil.* Psalm 119:1-7. Psalm 17:4.

(7) *Answered prayer.* John 15:7.

NOTE: Have the passages in the answers to the last question found and read without comment, as the closing exercise of the hour.

Book Hint. "The Printed English Bible" by Lovett is a cheap, attractive and fresh book. It gives, in a small space, much information regarding the way we got the Bible.

LESSON III.

Our God. The Father.

DAILY READINGS.

First Day........................... Matthew 5:1-16
Second Day........................ Matthew 6:1-18
Third Day.......................... Matthew 6:19-34
Fourth Day........................ Matthew 7:6-27
Fifth Day........................... John 5:30-47
Sixth Day........................... John 14:1-24
Seventh Day....................... John 17:1-26

MEMORY TEXT.

"To us there is one God, the Father, of whom are all things, and we in him; and one Lord Jesus Christ, by whom are all things, and we by him." 1 Cor. 8:6.

1. Who first taught men about the Fatherhood of God?

Jesus. The name in the sense in which we use it is not found in the Old Testament. It occurs nearly 300 *times in the New Testament.*

2. Where is the name most frequently found?

It occurs 180 *times in the Gospels. In John's Gospel* 120 *times. In Jesus' farewell address and prayer, John* 14-17, *it occurs* 48 *times. See daily readings for illustrations.*

3. Why is it important that men become acquainted with God?

"Acquaint now thyself with him and be at peace. Thereby good shall come to thee." Job 22:21.

"This is life eternal that they might know thee . . . and him whom thou didst send, Jesus Christ." John 17:3, R. V.

4. How only can men become acquainted with the Father?

"No man hath seen God at any time; the only begotten Son . . . he hath declared him." John 1:18.

"I am the way, the truth, and the life. No man cometh unto the Father but by me." John 14:6. See also John 8:19. John 10:37, 38.

5. What were some of Jesus' most important teachings about the Father?

(1) *His love for men.* See Matt. 5:45, John 3:16.

(2) *His desire for the worship of sincere men.* John 4:23, 24.

(3) *His willingness to hear and answer the prayers of His children.* Matt. 6:6, Matt. 7:11.

(4) *His willingness to forgive sin.* Matt. 6:12. See also Eph. 4:32, R. V.

(5) *Men may honor the Father in their lives.* Matt 5:16.

6. What was the chief purpose of Jesus in His life and teachings?

To lead men to love and trust His Father, as He manifested Him.

"God sent his Son into the world . . . that the world should be saved through him." John 3:17.

"This is the will of my Father, that everyone that beholdeth the Son, and believeth on him, should have eternal life." John 6:40, R. V. See also Psalm 37:40.

NOTE: The Parable of the Prodigal Son, Luke 15, is a striking illustration of this question.

7. What is the first step towards this love and trust in the Father?

An immediate turning away from sin, and acceptance of Jesus as Saviour and Lord.

"Those things which God foreshowed by the mouth of all the prophets, that his Christ should suffer, he hath thus fulfilled. Repent ye therefore and turn again that your sins may be blotted out." See Acts 3:18-19, R. V.

"Sirs, What must I do to be saved? And they said, Believe on the Lord Jesus Christ and thou shalt be saved." See Acts 16:27-34, 1 John 2:23.

8. How can child-like confidence in the Father be developed?

(1) *By prayer.* John 14:10-14.

(2) *By study of His Word.* Proverbs 22:17-21.

(3) *By daily practice.* 1 Peter 5:6-11.

LESSON IV.

Our God. The Exalted Son.

DAILY READINGS.

First Day........................John 3:19-36
Second Day......................John 4:1-26
Third Day.......................John 4:27-42
Fourth Day......................John 5:1-18
Fifth Day.......................John 5:19-29
Sixth Day ....Philippians 2:1-16
Seventh Day.......................Acts 1:1-11

MEMORY TEXT.

"This is my beloved Son, in whom I am well pleased: hear ye him." Matthew 17:5.

1. What are some of the titles of our Lord, and what do they signify?

(1) *"Jesus," His earthly name, given by the angel before His birth, means "Jehovah my salvation." Signifies His entire mission as Saviour of men.*

"His name shall be called Jesus, for he shall save his people from their sins." Matt. 1:21.

(2) *"Christ" means the "anointed one." The promised Messiah of the Old Testament prophecies.*

"God anointed him with the Holy Spirit and with power." Acts 10:38.
"Christ also suffered for us . . . . who bare our sins in his own body on the tree." 1 Peter 2:21-24. See also John 4:25, Acts 17:2, 3, R. V., Gal. 2:20.

(3) *"Master," or "Teacher," suggests His work of teaching while on earth the truth of God, about Himself, about man and his destiny.*

"One is your Master, even Christ." Matt. 23:10.

(4) *"Lord" means ruler or sovereign; suggests His rule in the hearts of His followers, and finally over the kingdoms of the world.*

"If thou shalt confess with thy mouth Jesus as Lord, and shalt believe in thine heart . . . thou shalt be saved." Rom. 10:10-13, R. V.

(5) *"Advocate" suggests His present work in the presence of God for His followers.*

"**We have an advocate with the Father, Jesus Christ the righteous.**" 1 John 2:1. See also Hebrews 9:24.

2. What important but mysterious fact should always be kept in mind regarding Jesus?

That He was and is the divine and yet human Jesus of Nazareth, Son of God, Son of Man.

"**There is one God and one mediator between God and men, himself man, Christ Jesus.**" 1 Timothy 2:5, R. V.

"**I and my Father are one.**" John 10:30.

3. How does a realization of His humanity help us?

It makes His sympathy with us in our temptations and weaknesses seem more real and practical.

"**For in that he hath suffered, being tempted, he is able to succor them that are tempted.**" Heb. 2:18.

"**We have not a high priest who cannot be touched with the feeling of our infirmities, but one that hath been in all points tempted like as we, yet without sin.**" Heb. 4:15, R. V.

4. What were the four chief things Jesus came to do?

(1) *To teach men of God and His love.* John 14:8-11. (See Lesson III., page 13.)

(2) *To show the folly of sin.* John 8:34-36.

(3) *To unfold God's plan for their lives.* Matt. 6:33, 16:24-27.

(4) *To provide for their present and eternal salvation.* John 11:25-26. Rom. 5:10, R. V.

5. What were the means of accomplishing the first three of these?

(1) *His life on earth.* John 1:1-4.

(2) *His spoken words.* John 8:21-36.

6. How did he make possible the fourth?

(1) *By His death and resurrection.* 1 Peter 1:3

(2) *By preserving a true account of His life and teachings and those of His chosen followers.* John 20:31. 2 Peter 1:15-19.

(3) *By imparting His own life to all who believe in Him.* John 10:27. 1 John 5:11.

(4) *By sending His Spirit to abide in the lives of all believers.* John 14:16, 17.

7. How is Jesus now helping His followers?

" Wherefore he is able to save unto the uttermost all who come unto God through him, seeing he ever liveth to make intercession for them." Heb. 7:25.

8. What is His chief desire for every man?

" Ye know the grace of our Lord Jesus Christ, that though he was rich, for your sakes he became poor, that ye through his poverty might be rich." 2 Cor. 8:9, 1 Tim. 2:4.

9. What is the main thing in the Christian life?

Personal, constant fellowship with the exalted Jesus. See Colossians 3:1-4, 1 John 1:3-7, 1 Peter 1:8.

LESSON V.

Our God. The Ever Present Helper.

DAILY READINGS.

First Day............................John 7:37-52
Second Day.........................John 14:15-26
Third Day...........................John 15:17-27
Fourth Day..........................John 16:1-14
Fifth Day.............................Acts 1:1-8
Sixth Day............................Acts 2:1-21
Seventh Day........................Acts 2:22-39

MEMORY TEXT.

" I will pray the Father and he shall give you another Helper that he may be with you forever." John 14:16, R. V., margin.

1. What was one of the last promises made by Jesus before His ascension?

   "Lo, I am with you alway, even unto the end of the age." Matt. 28:20. See R. V., margin.

2. What somewhat similar promise was made to His disciples the night before He was crucified?

   "I will not leave you comfortless—I will come to you." John 14:18. See also John 16:7.

3. How were these promises fulfilled?

   By the coming of the Holy Spirit or Comforter, or Helper (also called the Holy Ghost, the Spirit of God, the Spirit of Christ). See Romans 8:9-11.

4. Who is this Helper?

   God, as He manifests Himself in human lives. See the references to Him in the daily readings, which indicate His personality. See as illustrations Acts 13:1-4, *Acts* 5:1-3.

5. What does He do for men who have not become followers of Jesus?

   (1) *He convicts of sin.* John 16:8.

   (2) *He lifts up and makes Jesus attractive to men though the proclamation of the good news.* See John 15:26, John 16:14.

6. What does He do for a man after he becomes a follower of Jesus?

   (1) *Gives him a new heart.* (See Lesson VIII.)

   (2) *Puts the love of God into his heart.* Rom. 5:5.

   (3) *Helps him in prayer.* Rom. 8-26, 27.

   (4) *Helps him in every effort towards right living.* Phil. 2:12, 13.

   (5) *Helps him to understand the Word of God.* 1 Cor. 2:9-14.

   (6) *Gives him hope.* Rom. 15:13.

7. Does He dwell with every true believer in Jesus?

   "If any man hath not the Spirit of Christ he is none of his." Rom. 8-9, R. V. See also 1 Cor. 6:19, Ephesians 1:12-14, 2:21, 22, R. V.

8. How do Christians hinder His work in their lives?

(1) *By disobedience to Jesus' teachings.* John 14:15-17. 1 John 2: 4-6.

(2) *By harsh speaking and unkindness.* Eph. 4:29-32.

(3) *By neglecting known duties.*

9. What will be the result of giving this Mighty Helper the right of way in one's life?

He will develop a character more and more like that of Jesus, filling the life with gladness, and making it useful to men.

"We all with unveiled face, reflecting as in a mirror the glory of the Lord, are changed into the same image . . . . by the Lord, the Spirit." 2 Cor. 3:18, R. V.

"The fruit of the Spirit is love, joy, peace, long suffering, gentleness, goodness, faithfulness, meekness, self-control; against such there is no law." Gal. 5:22, 23, R. V.

10. What is the greatest attribute of God? *Love.*

(1) *God the Father loves us and wants us to become His children.* 2 Thess. 2:16, 1 John 3:1.

(2) *God the Son loved us, and died to make possible our becoming God's children.* Galatians 2:20, 3:26; Rom. 8:35.

(3) *God the Spirit loves us and comes to train us as God's children.* Romans 15:30.

Book Hint. "Plain Papers on the Holy Spirit," by Dr. Scofield, is a clear, simple, and practical little book on this great theme. See page 42.

LESSON VI.

Man: What He Is. What He Can Be.

DAILY READINGS.

First Day....Genesis 6:1-12
Second Day....Job 9:1-35
Third Day....Psalm 51:1-19
Fourth Day....Psalm 130:1-8
Fifth Day....Psalm 103:1-22
Sixth Day....Isaiah 53:1-12
Seventh Day....Romans 12:1-21

MEMORY TEXT.

"But now in Christ Jesus ye that once were afar off are made nigh in the blood of Christ." Eph. 2:13, R. V.

I.—MAN AS HE IS BY NATURE.

1. What are the sources of information regarding the nature and character of man?

   (1) *History—sacred and profane.*

   (2) *Personal study and observation.*

   (3) *Personal experience.*

2. How do they agree as to man's moral nature?

3. Why is God's Word the most reliable source of information regarding man's moral nature.

   (1) *It is impartial.*

   "For there is no respect of persons with God." Romans 2:11. 1 Peter 1:17.

   (2) *It is faithful to the facts.*

   "For all have sinned and come short of the glory of God." Rom. 3:23.

   (3) *It is absolutely truthful.*

   "Thy word is true from the beginning, and every one of thy righteous judgments endureth forever." Psalm 119:160.

   (4) *It is the product of divine love and sympathy.*

   "All scripture is given by inspiration of God, and is profitable for . . . instruction in righteousness." 2 Tim. 3:16.

   "He has granted unto us his exceeding great and precious promises: that by these ye may become partakers of a divine nature." 2 Peter 1:4, R. V.

4. What is its testimony regarding the natural man?

(1) *Has wandered from God and is in rebellion against His authority.*

"**All we like sheep have gone astray, we have turned every one to his own way.**" Isaiah 53:6.
"**The mind of the flesh is enmity against God.**" Romans 8:7, R. V. See also Jeremiah 17:9, John 3:19.

(2) *Unaided is incapable of righteous character.*

"**While we were yet without strength, in due time Christ died for the ungodly.**" Romans 5:6. See also Ephesians 4:18.

"**Dead in trespasses and sins.**" Ephesians 2:1. See verses 2, 3.

5. How does fallen human nature show itself?

(1) *By not believing God's* truth. John 3:18-20.

(2) *By evil thoughts and desires.*

"**Out of the heart proceed evil thoughts, murders, adulteries, fornications, thefts, blasphemies.**" Matthew 15:19. See also Gen. 6:5, Mark 7:21-23, Deuteronomy 32-18.

(3) *By evil deeds.* See Galatians 5:16-21.

(4) *By omitting right deeds.* James 4:17.

6. What are some results of this condition?

(1) *Corruption, suffering, lawlessness.* Isaiah 1:2-6.

(2) *Death—spiritual, physical.* Romans 6:23, 8:6-8.

(3) *The abiding wrath of God on all who reject Jesus.* John 3:36.

II.—MAN AS HE MAY BECOME.

7. What is God's three-fold desire for every man?
(1) *To forgive him.* (See Lesson VII.)

"That he by the grace of God should taste death for every man." Heb. 2:9.

(2) *To give him a fresh start.* (See Lesson VIII.)

(3) *To train him for useful service here and glory hereafter.* (See Lessons X to XII.)

8. What is God's pattern for each man's life?

   Jesus of Nazareth. See Romans 8:29, Ephesians 4:13.

9. What are some things which should characterize a saved man.

   (1) *A body dedicated to God, and developed for His glory.* Romans 12:1, 1 Corinthians 6:19, 20, R. V.

   (2) *A mind filled with pure thoughts.* 2 Corinthians 10:3-5, Phil. 4:8.

   (3) *The entire life devoted to Him.* John 12:26, Romans 12:1, 2.

10. Is such a life possible to every man?

    "There is no difference . . . for the same Lord over all is rich unto all that call upon him. For whosoever shall call upon the name of the Lord shall be saved." Romans 10:9-13.

    "Look unto me and be ye saved all ye ends of the earth." Isaiah 45:22.

LESSON VII.

Man: His Need. Forgiveness.

DAILY READINGS.

First Day.........................Psalm 32:1-11
Second Day....................Numbers 14:11-25
Third Day.........................Psalm 25:1-22
Fourth Day......................Isaiah 55:6-13
Fifth Day.........................Luke 23:32-43
Sixth Day..........................Acts 10:34-43
Seventh Day..................Romans 5:1-11

MEMORY TEXT.

" I, even I, am he that blotteth out thy transgressions for mine own sake, and will not remember thy sins." Isaiah 43:25.

I.—FORGIVENESS MADE POSSIBLE.

1. What are some of the words used to describe what God does with the sins of a truly penitent man?

   (1) *Pardons.* Isaiah 55:7.

   (2) *Forgives.* Ephesians 4:32.

   (3) *Remits.* Acts 10:43.

   (4) *Blots out.* Isaiah 44:22.

   (5) *Forgets.* Hebrews 8:12.

2. Do all these expressions mean the same thing?

3. Why will not God overlook the past and simply allow one to live a different life as a means of salvation?

It would be unjust to His character and to His revealed law. He must be just as well as gracious. He cannot be God and ignore sin. Romans 3:26., Habbakkuk 1:12,13.

4. How has God provided for the sinner's need?

" This is my blood of the new testament which is shed for many for the remission of sins." Matt. 26:28.

" Be it known unto you . . . men and brethren that through this man is preached unto you the fogiveness of sins." Acts 13:38.

" His dear Son, in whom we have redemption through his blood, even the forgiveness of sins." Col. 1:14. See also Isaiah 53:4-6.

II.—CONDITIONS OF FORGIVENESS.

5. What is the first thing necessary in order to forgiveness?

" Repent ye therefore and turn again that your sins may be blotted out." Acts 3:19, R. V. See also Luke 24:46, 47, Acts 26:20.

6. What does repentance mean?

The word literally mcans "change of mind," but its meaning in the Bible is much larger. It means a sufficient appreciation of what sin is to lead to a genuine sorrow on account of it, a hatred of it, and a willingness to immediately and forever turn from it.

7. What must accompany or follow genuine repentance in order to forgiveness?

The acceptance by faith of Jesus as God's appointed sacrifice for sin, and as the only Saviour and Lord.

"All have sinned and come short of the glory of God being justified (made right) freely by his grace through the redemption that is in Christ Jesus, whom God set forth to be a propitiation (or a sufficient offering) through faith by his blood." Rom. 3:23-25, R. V. See also Acts 10:43.

8. When does God forgive the penitent, seeking sinner who takes Jesus the best he knows how?

Immediately. See Luke 19:8-10, Luke 23:39-43.

9. What great blessings follow forgiveness?

(1) *Justification, or God's act of grace through which He treats the sinner as though he had not sinned.* See Rom. 4:25, 5:1.

(2) *Regeneration* (the new birth). (See Lesson VIII.) 2 Cor. 5:17.

(3) *The incoming of the Spirit of Christ to give victory over evil in the life.*

"Christ . . . in whom also after that ye believed, ye were sealed with that holy Spirit of promise." Ephesians 1:13.

"That Christ may dwell in your hearts by faith." Ephesians 3:17. See also Galatians 3:14, 4:4-7.

10. What should characterize one who has been forgiven?

(1) *Gratitude.* Psalm 103:1-3.

(2) *Gladness.* Psalm 32:1-2.

(3) *Whole-hearted devotion to Christ.* 2 Cor. 5:14, 15.

Note: Follow the suggestion of Lesson II. in having the references last given looked up and read aloud by the class just before the closing prayer.

LESSON VIII.

The Man: His Need. A New Heart.

DAILY READINGS.

First Day.........................Ezekiel 36:18-38
Second Day.........................John 1:1-13
Third Day.........................John 3:1-15
Fourth Day.........................1 Cor. 6:9-20
Fifth Day.........................2 Cor. 5:1-19
Sixth Day.........................1 Peter 1:3-25
Seventh Day.........................1 Peter 2:1-25

MEMORY TEXT.

"As many as received him to them gave he power to become the sons of God even to them which believe on his name." John 1:12.

I.—A GREAT CHANGE DESCRIBED.

1. What are the different words used to describe the great change which takes place when a man accepts Jesus as his Saviour?

(1) "*Conversion.*" *This means the turning of a man from the old to the new way, and includes, perhaps, all the various steps following repentance.*

"Except ye be converted (turn again) and become as little children, ye shall not enter into the kingdom of Heaven." Matt. 18:3.

(2) "*Regeneration.*" *It means literally another or a new birth.*

"Except a man be born anew he cannot see the kingdom of God." John 3:3, R. V. See Titus 3:3-5.

(3) *"A new heart" (not a "change of heart," which is unscriptural). This suggests God's gracious act in giving the sinner the seed of the new life.*

"A new heart will I give you and a new spirit will I put within you." Ezekiel 36:26.

"Create in me a clean heart, O God, and renew a right spirit within me." Psalm 51:10.

2. What is meant more than the cutting off of evil habits?

A radical and absolutely necessary change wrought by God, without which salvation is impossible.

"Ye must be born anew (or born from above)." John 3:5. See Matt. 15:19 for a reason.

II.—THE CHANGE ACCOMPLISHED.

3. Through what power is this great change brought about?

"Sons of God, . . . who were born not of blood nor of the will of the flesh, nor of the will of man, but of God." John 1:13. See John 3:5, Titus 3:5.

4. What is the instrument the Holy Spirit uses in bringing about this change?

"Born again . . . of incorruptible seed, through the word of God which liveth and abideth forever." 1 Peter 1:23. See James 1:18.

5. What is man's part in this great transaction?

To accept Jesus as Saviour and Lord by simple faith.

"Ye are all children of God by faith in Jesus Christ." Gal. 3:26. See John 1:12.

6. Does the change take place at the same time as the pardon of sins, and by the same act of faith?

Yes; when we accept Jesus we receive salvation, which includes all the blessings already described.

"Believe on the Lord Jesus Christ and thou shalt be saved." Acts 16:31.

III.—SOME RESULTS FOLLOWING THE CHANGE.

7. What striking expression does Paul use in 2 Cor. 5:17 to describe a regenerated man?

" If any man be in Christ he is a new creature; old things are passed away; behold, all things are become new."

8. What are some of the " new things?"

(1) *A new relationship to God—a son and heir.* Gal. 4:4-6.

(2) *A strong hatred of sin.* Rom. 7:15. 1 John 5:18.

(3) *A delight in God's law.* Rom. 7:22.

(4) *Victory over the world.* 1 John 5:4.

9. How can the new nature be made stronger?

(1) *By feeding daily on God's Word.*

" As new-born babes desire the sincere milk of his Word, ye may grow thereby." 1 Peter 2:2. (See Lesson XI.)

(2) *By daily fellowship with Jesus in prayer.*

Looking unto Jesus, the author and perfecter of our faith." Hebrews 12:2, R. V. (See Lesson X.)

(3) *By daily testimony for Jesus in life and word.*

" Go home to thy friends and tell them how great things the Lord hath done for thee." Mark 5:19. Find an illustration in Acts 9:19-22. (See Lesson XII.)

LESSON IX.

The Man. His New Life.

DAILY READINGS.

First Day	John 10:7-30
Second Day	John 11:1-27
Third Day	Acts 3:1-16
Fourth Day	Galatians 5:13-26
Fifth Day	Philippians 2:1-16
Sixth Day	1 Thess. 5:1-28
Seventh Day	Ephesians 3:14-21

MEMORY TEXT.

"I am come that they may have life and may have it abundantly." John 10:10, R. V.

I.—THE NEW LIFE DESCRIBED.

1. What are some of the words used to describe the new life of a man following his conversion?

(1) "*Sanctification.*" *It means to be set apart —dedicated to God.*

"Ye are washed, ye are sanctified . . . by the Spirit of our God." 1 Cor. 6:11. See Heb. 10:9, 10, 12:14, R. V.

(2) "*Holiness.*" *It literally means "wholeness," or soundness, a state of perfect spiritual health.*

"Let us cleanse ourselves from all filthiness of the flesh and spirit, perfecting holiness in the fear of God." 2 Cor. 7:1.

(3) "*Growth in grace.*" *Grace means the undeserved favor of God. To grow in grace is to let God's love more and more fill the life and control the conduct.*

"Grow in grace and in the knowledge of our Lord and Saviour Jesus Christ." 2 Peter 3:18.

2. What do these and similar expressions all refer to?

The results which should accompany the new life implanted in the believer by Jesus. Read with care 1 John 5:9-13, with Galatians 2:20.

3. What important facts should we constantly bear in mind regarding this new life?

(1) *Is in constant conflict with the "old man" —"the flesh." The two distinct natures remain to the end of life.* John 3:6, Romans 8:5-8, R. V. Gal. 5:17.

(2) *God who gave the new life will care for it.* Philippians 1:6, Romans 5:17, 1 Thess. 5:23.

(3) *The saved man should earnestly seek to develop the new life.* John 17:17. 1 Peter 3:15, R. V. Philippians 1:9-11.

II.—ITS PRACTICAL RESULTS.

4. What should be some results of this new life?

(1) *The possessor should put away every known sin.* Romans 6:12-14. Colossians 3:5-11.

(2) *Cultivate all the Christian graces, such as kindness, charity, and unselfishness.* Colossians 3:12-15.

(3) *Let Jesus control all plans, purposes, appetites, desires, habits, etc.* Colossians 3:16, 17, 23-25.

(4) *In a single word, he should develop strong, clean manhood.* Ephesians 4:1-3, 11-13, R. V; 1 Cor. 16:13.

5. What shall a man do with sins which he commits after beginning the Christian life?

Instantly repent, confess, and forsake them, and seek help to avoid repeating them.

" If we confess our sins, he is faithful and just to forgive us our sins." 1 John 1:9.

6. What should encourage a man who is fighting against sin within and without?

(1) *The sympathy of Jesus with his efforts.* Hebrews 4:15-16.

(2) *The help of God in every temptation.* 1 Cor. 10:13.

(3) *The sufficiency of the blood of Jesus to cleanse him.* Hebrews 9:11-14, 1 John 1:7.

(4) *The final, complete realization of his ideal through Jesus.* Hebrews 7:25, 1 John 3:1-3.

LESSON X.

Man: His Training. Prayer.

DAILY READINGS.

First Day	James 1:1-18
Second Day	James 5:13-20
Third Day	Luke 11:1-13
Fourth Day	Matthew 6:5-15
Fifth Day	Mark 11:15-25
Sixth Day	John 15:1-16
Seventh Day	Philippians 4:4-20

MEMORY TEXT.

"Let us draw near with boldness unto the throne of grace." Hebrews 4:16, R. V.

I.—THE IMPORTANCE OF PRAYER.

1. What facts make prayer so vital to a saved man?

(1) *His own weakness and ignorance.* Romans 7:18-24.

(2) *The forces of evil arrayed against him.* Ephesians 6:10-18.

(3) *The awful needs of the world.* 1 John 5:19.

2. In what other ways has its importance been emphasized?

(1) *By God's dealings with His people through the period of Old Testament history.* Psalm 62:8. Ezekiel 36:37.

(2) *By the teaching and example of Jesus.* Mark 1:35, Luke 6:12, 13; Luke 11:1-9.

(3) *By the teaching and example of the Apostles and early Christians.* Acts 1:12-14 12:5-17; Col. 1:3-9. *There are more than sixty references to prayer in Paul's writings.*

(4) *By the example of genuinely good men in every age.* See Ezra 9:3-6. 15; 1 Tim. 2:1-6.

II.—THE ENCOURAGEMENTS TO PRAY.

3. What is the greatest encouragement to pray?

The revealed character of God. Psalm 34:15-18, Matt. 6:6-8.

4. What are some of the further helps in prayer?

(1) *The abundant teaching of Jesus and the apostles. Fully 200 different passages in the New Testament on Prayer.*

(2) *The promised help of the Holy Spirit.* Romans 8:26, 27. See Eph. 6:18.

(3) *The experience of saved men in our time.*

III.—ELEMENTS OF SUCCESSFUL PRAYER.

5. What are some of the characteristics of effective prayer?

(1) *Desire.* Mark 11:24.

(2) *Faith.* Matt. 21:22.

(3) *Earnestness.* James 5:16.

(4) *Submission.* 1 John 5:14.

(5) *Perseverance.* Luke 18:1.

(6) *Obedience.* 1 John 3:22.

(7) *Unselfishness.* James 4:3.

6. Name some practical suggestions.

(1) *Be regular.* Have a daily time apart from the frequent moments of silent prayer.

(2) *Be definite.* Make a list of specific requests and bring them systematically before God.

(3) *Be studious.* Seek to learn more and more what the Bible teaches about prayer. It is worthy of the study of a lifetime.

(4) *Get alone as much as possible.* Find the secret place. Matt. 6:6.

(5) *Be thankful for answers received.* Philippians 4:6, 7.

7. In closing the hour let the class read in concert Psalm 91, and repeat together the Lord's Prayer.

NOTE: Leader and class should remember the avowed character of these studies. They simply touch the outer edge of these great truths. This lesson is a striking illustration of the fragmentary method. It will be valuable simply as a starting point.

LESSON XI.

The Saved Man: His Training. Bible Study.

DAILY READINGS.

First Day......................Deuteronomy 6:1-25
Second Day..........................John 5:30-47
Third Day.........................Hebrews 4:1-13
Fourth Day.........................Acts 17:1-15
Fifth Day.........................Acts 20:17-35
Sixth Day.........................Acts 28:17-31
Seventh Day.....................Nehemiah 8:1-12

MEMORY TEXT.

"Let the word of Christ dwell in you richly in all wisdom." Coll. 3:16.

I.—THE BASIS OF FRUITFUL BIBLE STUDY.

1. What is meant by Bible Study?

It is more than simply Bible reading. Study implies earnest, painstaking effort, according to some plan, with a definite end in view.

"They received the word with all readiness of mind and searched the scriptures daily, whether these things were so. Therefore many of them believed." Acts 17:11, 12.

2. Why is such study important?

(1) *Because the Bible contains the most important knowledge available to man.* Psalm 19:7-11.

(2) *Because most of its teachings cannot be comprehended by a superficial reading. They enter into the counsels of God. Therefore they deserve the best thought a man can put into them. The rich ore does not lie on the surface.* 2 Peter 3:14-16.

(3) *Because of the special benefits promised to sincere, diligent students.* James 1:21-25. Luke 24:32. (See Lesson II.)

3. What are some essential things in successful Bible study?

(1) *Confidence in the divine origin of the Bible.*

"Take the sword of the Spirit which is the word of God." Eph. 6:17. See John 2:22. 2 Tim. 3:15.

(2) *Earnestness and Patience.* Rom. 15:4. Phil. 3:8.

(3) *Dependence on God for help to grasp the meaning.*

"If any of you lack wisdom let him ask of God." James 1:5. See also John 14:26. Luke 24:45.

(4) *A willingness to obey the truth found.*

"**If any man willeth to do his will, he shall know of the teaching.**" John 7:17, R. V.

(5) *A definite purpose.*

"**Study to show thyself approved unto God . . . . rightly dividing (or handling aright) the word of truth.**" 2 Tim. 2:15.

II.—THE BEST AIM IN BIBLE STUDY.

4. Where do the most important teachings in the Bible centralize?

In the life and work of Jesus.

(1) *The Old Testament writings point forward to Him.* John 5:45-47. Luke 24:27, 44-48.

(2) *The Gospels record the facts of His earthly life and His teachings.*

(3) *The Acts tell of the founding of His Church to carry on His work.*

(4) *The letters comprise a manual of instruction for His Church.*

(5) *The Revelation tells of His glorious reign.*

"**The testimony of Jesus is the spirit of prophecy.**" Rev. 19:10.

5. What then should be the chief aim in Bible Study?

To learn about Jesus as He was, as He is, and as He will be, and find out how to become like Him. 2 Tim. 3:16, 17. I Peter 1:10, 11.

NOTE: A stimulating and suggestive pamphlet by Prof. McConaughy, entitled "Why read and study the Bible?" is commended to every student of this course. It costs 5 cents, and can be secured of the International Committee.

III.—SOME METHODS OF BIBLE STUDY.

6. Why is it important to follow some method in Bible Study?

(1) *To concentrate and hold the attention.*

(2) *To avoid shallowness.*

(3) *To insure definite progress.*

7. Name some of the practical methods.

(1) "*Study by Books," to ascertain the general character, purpose, contents, and authorship of the several Books of the Bible.*

NOTE: A Bible Dictionary and Sill's "Bible Study by Books" are valuable.

(2) "*Topical Study." Use Bible Text Book, Concordance, and marginal references.*

(3) "*Inductive Study." To ascertain from the book itself its general character, contents and teachings. First ascertain the facts, and from these form conclusions.*

NOTE: Several excellent Courses in this method are published by the International Committee.

(4) "*Biographical Study," or the study of Bible characters. In the life of Jesus use a good Harmony.*

8. What are desirable helps in Bible Study? *See page* 42, *noting especially Numbers* 1 to 6, 13 to 15.

NOTE: The leader should bring to the class copies of Concordance, Text Book, Bible Dictionary and Harmony, and explain their use.

9. What vital principle should always be remembered in reading and studying the Bible?

The Bible contains the personal message of my heavenly Father to me, his needy child, and should be reverently received and loyally obeyed. Psalm 78:1-7.

NOTE: Though the Bible contains the most important historical and geographical facts, teachings on political economy, and the oldest and choicest poetry in all literature, it is primarily the message of God to man. All else is incidental.

10. Indicate some practical hints for busy men.

(1) *Build up a Bible Library, beginning with a well-bound Bible, and Revised Testament.*

(2) *Decide at once to form and faithfully continue the habit of daily Bible reading and study, though you can only give a few minutes a day. Make your daily plans with this in view.*

(3) *If possible, give the daily reading the freshest moments, preferably in the morning.* Psalms 119:147.

(4) *Begin and close your study with prayer.*

"Open thou mine eyes." Psalms 119:18.

"Make me go in the path of thy commandments." Psalms 119:35.

(5) *When you find a good thing, "pass it on." Talk of your study with other men, and seek to enlist them.* Deuteronomy 6:6-9.

11. Read aloud in closing I Peter 2:1-10.

LESSON XII.

The Saved Man: His Training. Service.

READINGS.

First Day..........................John 1:29-45
Second Day..........................John 4:1-26
Third Day..........................John 4:27-45
Fourth Day..........................John 12:20-36
Fifth Day..........................Acts 8:26-40
Sixth Day..........................Acts 9:1-22
Seventh Day..........................I Thess. 1:1-10

MEMORY TEXT.

"Let him that heareth say, Come." Rev. 22:17.

I.—THE PURPOSE OF SALVATION.

1. What does Paul say as to the threefold purpose of Jesus in saving men? Titus 2:11-14, R. V.

(1) *To redeem them from all iniquity.*

(2) *To purify them for His own possession.*

(3) *To make them zealous in service.* See also 1 Peter 2:9-24, R. V.

2. Find in the daily readings illustrations of

   (1) *Witnessing for Christ with a relative.*

   (2) *Witnessing for Christ with a stranger.*

   (3) *Witnessing for Christ in public.*

3. How was Christianity originally established?

   By the testimony and service of redeemed men.

   "The Lord . . . was received up and sat down on the right hand of God, and they went forth and preached everywhere, the Lord working with them." Mark 16:19, 20. See also Acts 1:8, 4:10, 5:29-32.

4. How has it since been extended throughout the world?

   By the faithful efforts of Jesus' followers in every age. See 1 Thess. 1:2-9. Rom. 1:8, 16.

   "The Lord gave the word. Great was the company of those that published it." Psalm 68:11.

5. What follower is excused from service for His Master?

   See Memory Text, with Matt. 16:24. James 4:17.

II.—SOME KINDS OF SERVICE.

6. Name some of the most important ways of serving Christ.

   (1) *By confessing Him openly and uniting with His people.*

   "Everyone therefore who shall confess (acknowledge) me before men, him will I confess before my Father." Matt. 10:32, R. V. See Acts 2:47, 5:14.

   (2) *By helping to support and extend His cause in the world.* 2 Cor. 8:1-2, 9:6-8.

(3) *By living a consistent life "in the sphere of the daily calling."*

" Let your light so shine before men that they may see your good works and glorify your Father." Matt. 5:16. See Phil. 2:14-16. Col. 1:9-13.

(4) *By seeking opportunities to speak for Him.*

" Let the redeemed of the Lord say so." Psalm 107:2. See Psalm 119:46. John 4:39.

7. Why is personal testimony with individuals of peculiar value?

(1) *Men are more frank in personal conversation. Real hindrances are more easily met and overcome.*

(2) *Many men never attend public service. If they are ever reached, it must be by personal effort.*

(3) *Such service strengthens greatly the one who engages in it.*

(4) *It has the approval of Jesus in His precepts and example.* (See daily readings.)

(5) *Most saved men have been reached by personal effort.*

(6) *All followers of Christ can do it.*

8. What is essential in order to effective service?

(1) *Personal fellowship with Jesus.* John 1:35-42.

(2) *Personal acquaintance with His word.* 2 Tim. 3:16, 17.

(3) *The special help of the Holy Spirit.* 1 Cor. 2:9-16. 2 Cor. 3:4, 5.

9. What are some of the hindrances to personal effort?

(1) *Consciousness of wrong in one's own life.*

(2) *Cowardice—fear of ridicule.*

(3) *Sense of unfitness because of ignorance and inexperience.*

10. What is the greatest remedy for every hindrance?

A love for and trust in Jesus, developed by a growing acquaintance with Him and gratitude to Him.

"I can do all things through him who strengtheneth me." Phil. 4:13, 19, R. V.

"They overcame . . . by the blood of the Lamb and by the word of their testimony." Rev. 12:11.

11. How does the Bible describe those who help men into the Christian life?

"He that winneth souls is wise." Prov. 11:30.

12. How are they to be rewarded?

"They that be wise shall shine as the brightness of the firmament, and they that turn many to righteousness, as the stars forever and ever." Dan. 12:3.

13. Read aloud in closing the lesson, John 4:31-36. James 5:19, 20.

LESSON XIII.

The Man Redeemed. His Glorious Future.

DAILY READINGS.

First Day—Resurrection.............1 Cor. 15:1-34
Second Day—Resurrection...........1 Cor. 15:35-58
Third Day—Reunion..........1 Thess. 4:13-18, 5:1-11
Fourth Day—Reward..................Eph. 2:1-10
Fifth Day— " ....2 Cor. 5:1-10
Sixth Day— " ....2 Tim. 4:1-18
Seventh Day— " ....Rev. 22:1-21

MEMORY TEXT.

"Father, I will that they also whom thou hast given me be with me where I am, that they may behold thy glory." John 17:24.

I.—OUR HOPE. ITS FOUNDATION.

1. What three familiar words used by Paul suggest the greatest things in the Christian life?

"**Now abideth faith, hope, love.**" 1 Cor. 13:13, R. V.

2. How is each related to salvation?

(1) *Faith secures it.* Eph. 2:8.

(2) *Hope rejoices in it.* 1 Peter 1:3-8. Rom. 5:1-5.

(3) *Love manifests it.* 1 John 4:9-12.

3. What does hope mean?

It is a combination of earnest desire and reasonable expectation, and means more than either.

'**Hope putteth not to shame.**" Rom. 5:5, R. V.

"**We are saved in hope.**" Rom. 8:24, 25, R. V.

4. Where does the Christian's hope center?

"**Jesus Christ our hope.**" 1 Tim. 1:1.

"**Christ in you, the hope of glory.**" Col. 1:27.

5. On what is it founded?

The unchangeable character and unbreakable promises of God. Read Heb. 6:13-20.

II.—ITS SCOPE.

6. What is included in the Christian's hope?

(1) *He will see Jesus.* 1 John 3:1, 2. Rev. 22:4.

(2) *He will be united forever with all who have fallen asleep in Jesus.* 1 Thess. 4:14-17.

(3) *He will be made like Jesus, with a glorified body, at His coming.* Phil. 3:20, 21, R. V.

(4) *He will receive the reward of his service for Jesus.* 1 Cor. 3:10-14, R. V.

"**Behold I come quickly, and my reward is with me to give to every man according as his work shall be.**" Rev. 22:12.

7. What familiar word applied to a saved man finds its largest fulfillment in this hope?

" Beloved, now are we the sons of God." 1 John 3:2.

" If a son then an heir of God, through Christ." Gal. 4:7. See also Rev. 21:7.

III.—ITS PRACTICAL EFFECT.

8. What should be the practical results of the possession of this hope?

(1) *It should purify the life.*

" Every man that hath this hope set on him purifieth himself even as he is pure." 1 John 3:3. R. V.

(2) *Should make its possessor joyous.*

" The God of hope fill you with all joy and peace in believing, that ye may abound in hope, through the power of the Holy Spirit." Rom. 15:13.

(3) *Should lead to earnest, loyal service.* 1 Cor. 15:58. Col. 3:23, 24.

9. What is said of those who have not accepted Jesus as Saviour and Lord?

" Having no hope and without God in the world." Eph. 2:12. See 1 Thess. 4:13, R. V.

10. In the midst of the fight against sin within and without his own heart what great encouragement does this hope give to a saved man? Read James 1:12.

" Now unto him who is able to guard you from stumbling, and to present you faultless before the presence of his glory in exceeding joy, to the only wise God, our Saviour through Jesus Christ our Lord, be glory and majesty, dominion and power, before all time, and now and forevermore. Amen." Jude 24, 25, R. V.

LESSON XIV.

The Man. **Review.**

DAILY READINGS.

First Day	Ephesians	1:1-23
Second Day	"	2:1-22
Third Day	"	3:1-21
Fourth Day	"	4:1-32
Fifth Day	"	5:1-33
Sixth Day	"	6:1-24
Seventh Day	1 Corinthians	13:1-13

MEMORY TEXT.

"Watch ye; stand fast in the faith, quit you like men, be strong." 1 Cor. 16:13.

NOTE: In preparing for this lesson, read with care your own notes on Lessons VI-XIII. The review will help to fix the most important things in mind.

1. State three facts regarding the man who is not a Christian which show his sinfulness.
2. Indicate from these studies three passages of Scripture which tell of the results of sin.
3. Give two texts which indicate what God does with the sins of a man who repents and takes Jesus as his Saviour.
4. What great change takes place in the man who accepts Jesus as Saviour and Lord?
5. Give two Scripture texts which tell by whom the change is brought about.
6. Give one text which tells what means are used in accomplishing this change.
7. What three methods of training a converted man are considered in these studies?
8. Give one passage which emphasizes the importance of prayer.
9. Give one passage which contains a promise of answers to prayer.
10. Indicate three important conditions of answered prayer.
11. Give one text which emphasizes the central aim in Bible Study.
12. Describe one method of Bible study.

13. What is the purpose for which a man is saved? Give a passage to prove the answer.

14. What practical ways are suggested for serving God?

15. What are the rewards of faithful service for Jesus in this life? Give scriptural answer.

16. What should be the crowning thought in this and all studies of the Bible?

    To learn how to please God. Heb. 13:20,21, with John 8:26-30.

17. What is the source of power in our efforts to please God?

    "Let us lay aside every weight, and the sin which doth so easily beset us, and let us run with patience the race that is set before us, looking unto Jesus, the beginner and finisher of our faith; who for the joy set before him endured the cross, despising the shame, and is set down at the right hand of the throne of God. For consider him . . . lest ye be wearied and faint in your minds." Heb. 12:1-3.

www.ingramcontent.com/pod-product-compliance
Lightning Source LLC
Chambersburg PA
CBHW020231090426
42735CB00010B/1642

* 9 7 8 3 3 3 7 2 4 6 7 4 7 *